Musty-Crusty Animals

Lobsters

Lola M. Schaefer

Heinemann Library
Chicago, Illinois

Customer Service 888-454-2279
Visit our website at www.heinemannlibrary.com

Designed by Sue Emerson/Heinemann Library and Ginkgo Creative, Inc.
Printed and bound in the U.S.A. by Lake Book

06 05 04 03 02
10 9 8 7 6 5 4 3 2 1

Library of Congress Cataloging-in-Publication Data
Schaefer, Lola M., 1950-
   Lobsters / Lola Schaefer.
      p. cm —(Musty-crusty animals)
Includes index.
Summary: A basic introduction to lobsters, discussing their physical characteristics, habitat, diet, and activities.
   ISBN 1-58810-516-4 (lib. bdg.)   ISBN 1-58810-725-6 (pbk. bdg.)
   Lobster—Juvenile literature. [1. Lobsters.] I. Title.
   QL444.M33 S35 24 2002
   595.3'84—dc21

2001003285

Acknowledgments
The author and publishers are grateful to the following for permission to reproduce copyright material:
Title page, pp. 5, 10, 22 E. R. Degginger/Color Pic, Inc.; p. 4 Jane Burton/Bruce Coleman Inc.; p. 6 Marty Snyderman/ Visuals Unlimited; pp. 7, 13, 14, 15, 20 Jeff Rotman Photography; p. 8 Jonathan Bird; p. 9 Robert E. Barber; p. 11 Bryan Hitchcock/National Audubon Society/Photo Researchers, Inc.; p. 12 Jonathan Bird/ORG; p. 16 Doug Perrine/Jeff Rotman Photography; p. 17 Andrew J. Martinez/Photo Researchers, Inc.; p. 18 Zig Leszczynski/Animals Animals; p. 19 Michele Hall/Howardhall.com; p. 21 George D. Lepp/Photo Researchers, Inc.

Cover photograph courtesy of Jane Burton/Bruce Coleman Inc.

Every effort has been made to contact copyright holders of any material reproduced in this book. Any omissions will be rectified in subsequent printings if notice is given to the publisher.

Special thanks to our advisory panel for their help in the preparation of this book:

Eileen Day, Preschool Teacher
Chicago, IL

Paula Fischer, K–1 Teacher
Indianapolis, IN

Sandra Gilbert,
Library Media Specialist
Houston, TX

Angela Leeper,
Educational Consultant
North Carolina Department
of Public Instruction
Raleigh, NC

Pam McDonald, Reading Teacher
Winter Springs, FL

Melinda Murphy,
Library Media Specialist
Houston, TX

Helen Rosenberg, MLS
Chicago, IL

Anna Marie Varakin,
Reading Instructor
Western Maryland College

Special thanks to Dr. Randy Kochevar of the Monterey Bay Aquarium for his help in the preparation of this book.

Some words are shown in bold, **like this.**
You can find them in the picture glossary on page 23.

Contents

What Are Lobsters?

Lobsters are sea animals without bones.

They are **invertebrates**.

jointed leg

Lobsters have **jointed legs**.

The legs are for walking and holding food.

Where Do Lobsters Live?

Very young lobsters float in the ocean.

Later, they live on the ocean floor.

Some lobsters live in rocky holes.

They live alone or with other lobsters.

What Do Lobsters Look Like?

tail

Lobsters look like giant bugs.

They have long bodies and tails.

antennae

Lobsters have long **antennae** to feel, smell, and taste food.

Lobsters can be many different colors.

Do Lobsters Really Have Shells?

People call the hard outsides of lobsters "shells."

But lobster shells are really **exoskeletons.**

old shell

As lobsters grow, their shells get too small.

Then, they grow new, bigger shells.

What Do Lobsters Feel Like?

Lobsters feel crusty.

Their shells are bumpy and hard.

claw

Lobster **claws** feel sharp.

How Big
Are Lobsters?

Young lobsters are smaller than a penny.

Adult lobsters can be almost as big as a woman!

How Do Lobsters Move?

Lobsters crawl on the ocean floor.

Some lobsters crawl many miles.

tail

Lobsters can quickly curl their tails.

This moves them backwards.

What Do Lobsters Eat?

Lobsters eat soft foods.

They eat fish, worms, and seaweed.

sea star

Lobsters eat sea animals.

They eat clams and sea stars.

Where Do New Lobsters Come From?

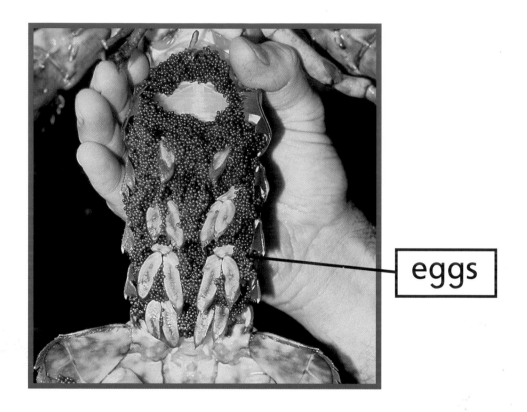

eggs

Female lobsters lay thousands of eggs.

The eggs stay on their tails for many months.

Then, the eggs float away.

Young lobsters come out of
the eggs.

Quiz

What are these lobster parts?

Can you find them in the book?

Look for the answers on page 24.

? ? ? ?

Picture Glossary

antennae
(an-TEN-ee)
page 9

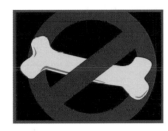
invertebrate
(in-VUR-tuh-brate)
page 4

claw
page 13

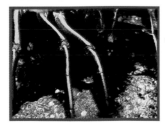
jointed legs
page 5

exoskeleton
(EX-oh-SKEL-uh-tuhn)
page 10

Note to Parents and Teachers

Reading for information is an important part of a child's literacy development. Learning begins with a question about something. Help children think of themselves as investigators and researchers by encouraging their questions about the world around them. Each chapter in this book begins with a question. Read the question together. Look at the pictures. Talk about what you think the answer might be. Then read the text to find out if your predictions were correct. Think of other questions you could ask about the topic, and discuss where you might find the answers. Assist children in using the picture glossary and the index to practice new vocabulary and research skills.

 CAUTION: Remind children that it is not a good idea to handle wild animals. Children should wash their hands with soap and water after they touch any animal.

Index

Answers to quiz on page 22

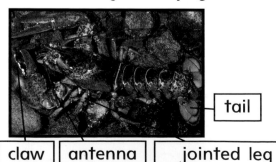

tail

claw   antenna   jointed leg